NETS by Jen Bervin

Ugly Duckling Presse, 2004
11th printing, 2019

ISBN 978-0-972768-43-6

Distributed by
SPD / Small Press Distribution,
Inpress Books (UK), and
Raincoast Books (Canada)
via Coach House Books

THE SON**NETS** OF WILLIAM SHAKESPEARE

JEN BERVIN

For Will—hold me to my name.

THE SONNETS OF WILLIAM SHAKESPEARE

When forty winters shall beseige thy brow,
And dig deep trenches in thy beauty's field,
Thy youth's proud livery, so gazed on now,
Will be **a** tattered **weed, of small worth** held:
Then being **asked** where all thy beauty lies,
Where all the treasure of thy lusty days,
To say, within thine own deep-sunken eyes,
Were an all-eating shame and thriftless praise.
How much more praise deserved thy beauty's use,
If thou couldst answer 'This fair child of mine
Shall sum my count and make my old excuse,'
Proving his beauty by succession thine.
This were **to be new made** when thou art old,
And see thy blood warm when thou feel'st it cold.

Look in thy glass and tell the face thou viewest
Now is the time that face should **form another**;
Whose **fresh repair** if now thou not renewest,
Thou dost beguile the world, unbless some mother.
For where is she so fair whose uneared womb
Disdains **the tillage** of thy husbandry?
Or who is he so fond will be the tomb
Of his self-love to stop posterity?
Thou art thy mother's glass, and she in thee
Calls back the lovely April **of** her prime;
So thou through **windows** of thine age shalt see,
Despite of wrinkles, this thy golden time.
    But if thou live remembered not to be,
    Die **single, and thine** image dies with thee.

Those **hours** that with gentle work did frame
The lovely gaze where every eye doth dwell
Will play the tyrants to the very same
4   And that unfair which fairly doth excel;
For never-resting Time leads summer on
To hideous winter and confounds him there;
Sap checked with frost **and** lusty leaves quite gone,
8   Beauty o'ersnowed and **bareness** everywhere.
Then, were not summer's distillation left
A liquid prisoner pent in walls of glass,
Beauty's effect with beauty were bereft,
12   Nor it nor no remembrance what it was.
But flowers **distill**ed, though they with winter meet,
Leese but their show; **their substance** still lives sweet.

Music to hear, why hear'st thou music sadly?
Sweets with sweets war not, joy delights in joy;
Why lov'st thou that which thou receiv'st not gladly,
Or else receiv'st with pleasure thine annoy?
If the true concord of well-tunèd sounds,
By unions married, do offend thine ear,
They do but sweetly chide thee, who confounds
In singleness the parts that thou shouldst bear.
Mark how one string, sweet husband to another,
Strikes **each in each** by mutual ordering;
Resembling sire, and child, and happy mother,
Who all in one, one pleasing note do sing;
    Whose **speechless song, being many, seeming one**,
    Sings this to thee: 'Thou single wilt prove none.'

As fast as thou shalt wane, so fast thou grow'st
In one of thine from that which thou departest;
And that fresh blood which youngly thou bestow'st
4 Thou mayst call thine, when thou from youth convertest.
Herein lives wisdom, beauty, and increase;
Without this, folly, age and cold decay.
If all were minded so, the times should cease
8 And threescore year would make the world away.
Let those whom Nature hath not made for store
Harsh, featureless, and rude—barrenly perish.
Look whom she best endowed **she gave the more**,
12 Which bounteous gift thou shouldst in bounty cherish.
    She carved thee for her seal, and meant thereby
    Thou shouldst print more, not let that copy die.

When I do **count the** clock that tells the time,
And see the brave day sunk in hideous night;
When I behold the violet past prime,
4 And sable curls all silvered o'er with white;
When lofty **trees** I see barren of leaves,
Which erst from heat did canopy the herd,
And summer's **green**, all **girded up in sheaves**,
8 Borne on the bier with white and bristly beard;
Then of thy beauty do I question make,
That thou among the wastes of time must go,
Since sweets and beauties do themselves forsake,
12 And die as fast as they see others grow;
    And nothing 'gainst Time's scythe can make defence
    Save breed to brave him when he takes thee hence.

13

O that you were **yourself**; but, love, you are
No longer yours than you yourself here live.
Against this coming end you should prepare,
And your sweet semblance to some other give.
So should that beauty which you hold in lease
Find no determination; then you were
Yourself **again after** yourself's decease,
When your sweet issue your sweet **form** should bear.
Who **lets** so fair **a house fall to** decay,
Which husbandry in honour might up**hold**
Against the stormy gusts of winter's day

And barren rage of death's eternal cold?
    O, none but unthrifts! Dear my love, **you** know
    You had a father; let your son say so.

Not from the stars do I my judgment pluck,
And yet methinks I have astronomy;
But not to tell of good or evil luck,
4   Of plagues, of dearths, or seasons' quality;
Nor can I fortune to brief minutes tell,
Pointing to each his thunder, rain, and wind,
Or say with princes if it shall go well
8   By oft predict that I in heaven find.
But from thine eyes my knowledge I derive,
And, **constant** stars, in them I read such art
As truth and beauty shall together thrive
12   If **from** thyself to store thou wouldst convert;
    Or else of thee **this** I prognosticate,
    Thy end is truth's and beauty's doom and **date**.

When I consider every thing that grows
Holds in perfection but a little moment,
That this huge stage presenteth naught but shows
Whereon **the stars** in secret influence comment;
When I perceive that men as plants increase,
Cheerèd and checked even by **the selfsame sky**,
Vaunt in their youthful sap, at height decrease,
And wear their brave state out of memory;
Then the conceit of this inconstant stay
Sets you most rich in youth before my sight,
Where wasteful Time debateth with Decay,
To change your day of youth to sullied night;
    And all in war with Time **for love of you**,
    As he takes from you I engraft you new.

But wherefore do not you a mightier way
Make war upon this bloody tyrant Time,
And fortify yourself in your decay

4   With means more blessèd than my barren rhyme?
Now stand you on the top of happy hours,
And many maiden gardens, **yet unset**,
With virtuous wish would bear **your** living flowers,

8   Much liker than your painted counterfeit.
So should the **lines of** life that life **repair**,
Which this time's pencil or my pupil pen
Neither in **inward** worth **nor outward** fair

12   Can make you live yourself in eyes of men.
    To give away yourself keeps yourself still,
    And you must live **drawn** by your own sweet skill.

2

18 ·

Shall I compare thee to a summer's day?
Thou art more lovely and more temperate.
Rough winds do shake the darling buds of May,
4   And summer's lease hath all too short a date.
Sometime too hot the eye of heaven shines,
And often is his gold complexion dimmed;
And every fair from fair sometime declines,
8   By chance or nature's changing course untrimmed;
But thy eternal summer shall not fade,
Nor lose possession of that fair thou ow'st,
Nor shall Death brag **thou wand'rest in** his **shade**,
12   When **in** eternal **lines to time** thou grow'st.
　　So long as men can breathe or eyes can see,
　　So long lives this and this gives life to thee.

A woman's face with Nature's own hand painted,
Hast thou, the **master-mistress of my** passion;
A woman's gentle heart, but not acquainted
4   With **shifting** change, as is false women's fashion;
An eye more bright than theirs, less false in rolling,
Gilding the object whereupon it gazeth;
A man in hue all hues in his controlling,
8   Which steals men's eyes and women's souls amazeth.
And for a woman wert thou first created,
Till Nature as she wrought thee fell a-doting,
And **by** addition me of thee defeated,
12   By **adding** one thing to my purpose **nothing**.
    But since she **prick'd thee out for** women's **pleasure**,
    Mine be thy love, and thy love's use their treasure.

So is it not with me as with that Muse,
Stirred by a painted beauty to his verse,
Who heaven itself for ornament doth use,
And every fair with his fair doth rehearse,
Making a couplement of proud compare
With sun and moon, with earth and sea's rich gems,
With April's first-born flowers, and **all things rare**
That heaven's air in this huge rondure hems.
O let me, true in love, but truly write,
And then, believe me, my love is as fair
As any mother's child, though not so bright
As those gold candles **fixed in** heaven's **air**.
    Let them say more that like of hearsay well;
    I will not praise that purpose not to sell.

My glass shall not persuade me **I am** old
So long as youth and thou are **of one date**;
But when **in** thee **time's furrows** I behold,
Then look I death my days should expiate.
For all that beauty that doth cover thee
Is but the seemly raiment of my heart,
Which in thy breast doth live, as thine in me:
How can I then be elder than thou art?
O, therefore, love, be of thyself so wary
As I, not for myself, but for thee will,
Bearing thy heart, which I will keep so chary
As tender nurse her babe from faring ill.
    Presume not on thy heart when mine is slain;
    Thou gav'st me thine, not to give back again.

23

As **an unperfect** actor on the stage,
Who with his fear is put besides his **part,**
Or **some fierce** thing replete with too much rage,
4   Whose **strength's** abundance weakens his own heart;
So I, for fear of trust, forget to say
The perfect ceremony of love's rite,
And in mine own love's strength seem to decay,
8   O'ercharged with burden of mine own love's might.
O, let my books be then the eloquence
And dumb **presager**s of my speaking breast,
Who plead for love and look for recompense
12   More than that tongue that more hath more expressed.
    O, learn to read what silent love hath writ;
    To hear with eyes belongs to love's fine wit.

Mine eye hath played the painter and hath **stell'd**
Thy beauty's form in table of my heart;
My body is the frame wherein 'tis held,
4   And **perspective** it is the painter's art,
For **through** the painter must you see his skill
To find where your true image pictured lies,
Which in my bosom's shop is hanging still,
8   That hath his **windows glazed with** thine eyes.
Now see what good turns eyes for **eyes** have done:
Mine eyes have drawn thy shape, and thine for me
Are windows to my breast, wherethrough the sun
12 Delights to peep, to gaze therein on thee.
    Yet eyes this cunning want to grace their art;
    They draw but what they see, know not the heart.

26

Lord of my love, **to** whom in vassalage
Thy merit hath my duty strongly **knit**,
To thee I send this written embassage,
To witness duty, not to show my wit—
Duty so great, which wit so poor as mine
May make seem **bare, in wanting** words to show it,
But **that** I **hope** some good conceit of thine
In thy soul's thought, all naked, **will bestow it**,
Till whatsoever star that guides my moving
Points on me graciously with fair aspect,
And puts apparel on my tattered loving,
To show me worthy of thy sweet respect.
    Then may I dare to boast how I do love thee,
    Till then not show my head where thou mayst prove me.

Weary with toil, I haste me to my bed,
The dear repose for limbs with travel tired;
But then begins a journey in my head

4   To work my mind when body's work's expired;
For then my thoughts, from far where I abide,
Intend a zealous **pilgrimage to thee**,
And keep my drooping eyelids open wide,

8   Looking on darkness which the blind do see;
Save that my soul's imaginary sight
Presents thy shadow to my sightless view,
Which like a jewel hung in ghastly night,

12   **Makes black night beauteous and her** old face new.
Lo, thus, by day my **limbs, by night my mind**,
For thee and for myself, no quiet find.

How can I then return in happy plight
That am debarred the benefit **of** rest,
When day's oppression is not eased by night,
4   But day by night and night by day oppressed,
And each, though enemies to either's reign,
Do in consent shake **hands** to torture me,
The one by toil, the other to complain
8   How far I toil, **still farther off** from thee?
I tell the day, to please him thou art bright
And dost him grace when **clouds** do blot the heaven;
So flatter I the swart-complexioned night,
12 When sparkling stars twire not, thou gild'st the even.
      But day doth daily draw my sorrows longer,
      And night doth nightly make grief's strength seem stronger.

When, in disgrace with fortune and men's eyes,
I all alone beweep my **outcast** state,
And trouble deaf heaven with my bootless cries,
4   And look upon myself and curse my fate,
Wishing me like to one more rich in hope,
Featured like him, like him with friends possessed,
Desiring this man's art, and that man's scope,
8   With what I most enjoy contented least;
Yet, in these **thoughts** myself almost despising,
Haply I think on thee, and then my state,
Like to the lark at **break** of day arising
12 From sullen earth, sings hymns at heaven's gate;
    For thy sweet love remembered such wealth brings
    That then I scorn **to change my state** with kings.

33

Full many a glorious morning have I seen
Flatter the mountain-tops with sovereign eye,
Kissing with golden face the meadows green,
4   Gilding pale streams with heavenly alchemy,
Anon permit the basest clouds to ride
With ugly rack on his celestial face,
And from the forlorn world his visage hide,
8   Stealing **unseen** to west with this disgrace.
Even so my sun one early morn did shine
With all triumphant **splendor** on my brow;
But out, alack, he was but **one hour mine**,
12 **The region cloud** hath mask'd him from me now.
    Yet him for this my love no whit disdaineth;
    Suns of the world may stain when heaven's sun staineth.

Why didst thou promise such a beauteous day
And make me travel forth without my cloak,
To let base clouds **o'ertake me** in my way,
4   Hiding thy brav'ry in their rotten smoke?
'Tis not enough that through the cloud thou **break**
To dry the rain on my storm-beaten face,
For no man well of such a salve can speak
8   That heals the wound and cures not the disgrace.
Nor can thy shame give physic to my grief;
Though thou repent, yet I have still the loss.
Th'offender's sorrow lends but weak relief
12   To him that bears the strong offence's cross.
    Ah, but those **tear**s are pearl which thy love **sheed**s,
    And they are rich and ransom all ill deeds.

No more be grieved at that which thou hast done:
Roses have thorns, and silver fountains mud,
Clouds and **eclipses** stain both moon and sun,
4   And loathsome canker lives in sweetest bud;
All men make faults, and even I in this
Authorizing thy trespass with compare,
Myself corrupting, salving thy amiss,
8   Excusing thy sins more than thy sins are;
For to thy sensual fault I bring **in sense**—
(Thy adverse party is thy advocate)
And 'gainst myself a lawful plea commence.
12   Such civil war is in my love **and** hate
        That I an accessary **need**s must be
        To that sweet thief which sourly robs from me.

How can my Muse want subject to invent,
While thou dost breathe, that **pour**'st into my verse
Thine own sweet argument, too excellent
4   For every vulgar paper to rehearse?
O, give thyself the thanks, if aught **in** me
Worthy perusal stand against thy sight;
For who's so dumb that cannot write to thee,
8   When thou thyself dost give invention **light**?
Be thou the tenth Muse, ten times more in worth
Than those old nine which rhymers invocate;
And he that calls on thee, let him bring forth
12   Eternal numbers to outlive long date.
    If my slight Muse do please **these curious days**,
    The pain be mine, but thine shall be the praise.

If the dull substance of my flesh were thought,
Injurious distance should not stop my way;
For then despite of **space** I would be brought,
4   From limits **far remote, where** thou dost stay.
No matter then although my foot did stand
Upon the farthest earth removed from thee;
For nimble thought can jump both **sea and land**
8   As soon as **think the** place where he would be.
But ah, thought kills me that I am not thought,
To leap large **lengths of** miles when thou art gone,
But that, so much of earth and water wrought,
12   I must attend time's leisure with my moan;
    Receiving naught by **elements so slow**
    But heavy tears, badges of either's woe.

45

The other two, slight air and purging fire,
Are both with thee, wherever I abide;
The first **my thought**, the other **my desire**,
These **present-absent** with swift motion slide.
For when these quicker elements are gone
In tender embassy of love to thee,
My life, being made of four, with two alone
Sinks down to death, oppressed with melancholy;
Until life's composition be recured
By those swift messengers return'd from thee,
Who even but now come back again, assured
Of thy fair health, recounting it to me.
   This told, I joy, but then no longer glad,
   I send them back again, and straight grow sad.

Against that time—if ever that time come—
When I shall see thee frown on my defects,
Whenas thy love hath cast his utmost sum
4   Called to that audit by advised respects;
Against that time when thou shalt strangely pass,
And scarcely greet me with that sun, thine eye,
When love, converted from the thing it was,
8   Shall reasons find of settled gravity;
Against that time do I ensconce me here
Within the knowledge of **mine own desert,**
And **this** my **hand against myself** uprear
12   To guard the lawful reasons on thy part.
    To leave poor me thou hast the strength of laws,
    Since why to love I can allege no cause.

So am I as the rich whose blessèd key
Can bring him to his sweet up-lockèd treasure,
The which he will not every hour survey,
For blunting the fine point of seldom pleasure.
Therefore are feasts **so solemn and so rare**,
Since, seldom coming, in the long year set,
Like stones of worth they thinly placèd are,
Or captain jewels in the carcanet.
So is the time that keeps you as my chest,
Or as the wardrobe which the robe doth hide,
To make some special instant special blest,
By new unfolding his imprisoned pride.
    Blessed are **you, who**se worthiness gives scope,
    Being **had**, **to** triumph, being lack'd, to **hope**.

53

What is your substance, whereof are you made,
That **millions of strange shadows** on you tend?
Since every one hath, every one, one shade,
And you, but one, can every shadow lend.
Describe Adonis, and the counterfeit
Is poorly imitated after you;
On Helen's cheek all art of beauty set,
And you in Grecian tires are painted new:
Speak of the spring and **foison of** the year;
The one doth shadow of your beauty show,
The other as your bounty doth appear,
And you in **every** blessed **shape we know**.
    In all external grace you have some part,
    But you like none, none you, for constant heart.

55

Not marble nor the gilded monuments
Of princes, shall outlive this powerful rhyme,
But you shall shine more bright in these contents
4   Than unswept stone, besmeared with **sluttish** time.
When **wasteful war** shall statues overturn,
And broils root out the work of masonry,
Nor Mars his sword nor war's quick fire shall burn
8   The living record of your memory.
'Gainst death and all-oblivious enmity
Shall **you** pace forth; your praise shall still find room
Even in the eyes of all posterity
12   That **wear this world out** to the ending doom.
        So, till the judgment that yourself arise,
        You live in this, and dwell in lover's eyes.

Like as the waves make towards the pebbled shore
So do our minutes hasten to their end;
Each changing place with that which goes before,
4   In sequent toil all forwards do contend.
Nativity, once in the main of **light**,
Crawls to maturity, wherewith being crowned,
Crookèd elipses 'gainst his glory fight,
8   And Time that gave doth now his gift confound.
Time doth transfix the flourish set on youth
And **delves the parallels** in beauty's brow,
Feeds on **the rarities** of nature's truth,
12   And nothing stands but for his scythe to mow.
   And yet to times in hope my verse shall stand,
   Praising thy worth, despite his cruel hand.

61

Is it thy will thy image should keep open
My heavy eyelids to the weary night?
Dost thou desire my **slumbers** should be **broken**,
While shadows like to thee do mock my sight?
Is it thy spirit that thou send'st from thee
So far from home into my deeds to pry,
To find out shames and idle hours in me,
The scope and tenor of thy jealousy?
O, no, thy love, though much, is not so great;
It is my love that keeps mine eye awake,
Mine own true love that doth my rest defeat,
To play the watchman ever for thy sake.
For thee watch I, whilst thou dost **wake elsewhere**,
From me **far off, with others** all too near.

63

Against my love shall be as **I am** now
With Time's injurious hand crushed and o'er worn;
When hours have drained his blood and filled his brow
4   With lines and wrinkles; when his youthful morn
Hath travelled on to age's steepy night,
And all those beauties whereof now he's king
Are **vanishing or vanished** out of sight,
8   Stealing away the treasure of his spring;
For such a time do I now fortify
Against confounding age's cruel knife,
That he shall never cut from memory
12 My sweet love's beauty, though my lover's life:
His beauty shall **in these black lines** be seen,
And they shall live, and he in them still green.

64

When **I have seen** by Time's fell hand defaced
The rich proud cost of outworn buried age,
When sometime lofty **towers** I see **down-razed**,
4   And brass eternal slave to mortal rage;
When I have seen the hungry ocean gain
Advantage on the kingdom of the shore,
And the firm soil win of the wat'ry main,
8   Increasing store with **loss** and **loss** with store;
When I have seen such interchange of state,
Or state itself confounded to decay,
Ruin hath taught me thus to ruminate—
12   That Time will come and take my love away.
       This thought is as a death, which cannot choose
       But weep to have that which it fears to lose.

()

Thus is his cheek the **map** of days outworn,
When beauty lived and died as flowers do now,
Before the bastard signs of fair were born,
4 Or durst inhabit on a living brow;
Before the golden tresses of **the** dead,
The right of sepulchres, were **shorn away**
To live a second life on second head—
8 Ere beauty's dead fleece made another gay.
In him those holy antique hours are seen
Without all ornament, itself and true,
Making no summer of another's green,
12 Robbing no old to dress his beauty new;
  And him as for a **map** doth Nature store,
  To show false Art **what beauty was** of yore.

69

Those parts of thee that the world's eye doth view
Want nothing **that** the thought of hearts can **mend**;
All tongues, the voice of souls, give thee that due,
Uttering bare truth, even so as foes commend.
Thy outward thus with outward praise is crowned;
But those same tongues that give thee so thine own
In other accents do this praise confound
By seeing **farther than** the eye hath shown.
They look into the beauty of thy mind,
And that in guess they **measure** by thy deeds;
Then, churls, their thoughts (although their eyes were kind)
To thy fair flower add the rank smell of weeds:
    But why thy odour matcheth not thy show,
    The soil is this—that thou dost common grow.

So shall I live, supposing thou art true,
Like a deceivèd husband; so love's face
May still seem love to me, though altered new,
4   Thy looks with me, thy heart in other place.
For there can live no **hatred in** thine eye,
Therefore in that I cannot know thy change.
In many's looks, **the** false **heart's history**
8   **Is writ** in moods and frowns and wrinkles **strange**.
But heaven in thy creation did decree
That in thy face sweet love should ever dwell;
Whate'er thy thoughts or thy heart's workings be,
12   Thy looks should nothing thence but sweetness tell.
    How like Eve's apple doth thy beauty grow,
    if thy sweet virtue answer not thy show!

How sweet and lovely dost thou make the shame
Which, like a canker in the fragrant rose,
Doth spot the beauty of thy budding name!
4   O, in what sweets dost thou thy sins enclose!
That tongue that tells the story of thy days,
Making lascivious comments on thy sport,
Cannot dispraise but in a kind of praise;
8   Naming thy name blesses an ill report.
O, what a mansion have those vices got
Which for their habitation chose out thee,
Where beauty's veil doth cover every blot,
12   And all things turn to fair that eyes can see!
    Take heed, dear heart, of this large privilege;
    The hardest knife ill-used doth lose his edge.

Some say thy fault is youth, some wantonness,
Some say thy grace is youth and gentle sport;
Both grace and faults are loved of more and less;
4   Thou mak'st faults graces that to thee resort.
As on the finger of a thronèd queen
The basest jewel will be well esteem'd,
So are **those errors** that in thee are seen
8   To truths **translated** and **for true** things deemed.
How many lambs might the stern wolf betray,
If like a lamb he could his looks **translate**,
How many gazers might'st thou lead away,
12   If thou wouldst use the strength of all thy state!
     But do not so; I love thee in such sort
     As, thou being mine, mine is thy good report.

How like a winter hath my absence been
From thee, the pleasure of the fleeting year!
What freezings have I felt, what dark days seen—
4   What old December's bareness everywhere!
And yet this time removed was summer's time,
The teeming autumn, big with rich increase,
Bearing the wanton burden of the prime,
8   Like widowed wombs after their lords' decease:
Yet this abundant issue seem'd to me
But hope of orphans and unfathered fruit;
For summer and his pleasures wait on thee,
12   And, thou away, **the very birds are mute**;
    Or, if they sing, 'tis with so dull a cheer
    That **leaves look pale**, dreading the winter's near.

From **you** have I been **absent in** the spring,
When proud-pied April dressed in all his trim,
Hath put a spirit of youth in **every thing**,
4   That heavy Saturn laughed and leaped with him.
Yet nor the lays of birds, nor the sweet smell
Of different flowers in odour and in hue,
Could make me any summer's story tell,
8   Or from their proud lap pluck them where they grew.
Nor did I wonder at the lily's white,
Nor praise **the deep vermilion** in the rose;
They were but sweet, but **figures** of delight,
12   Drawn after you, you **pattern of** all those.
        Yet seemed it winter still, and, you away,
        As with **your shadow** I with these did play.

The **forward violet** thus did I chide:
'Sweet thief, whence didst thou steal thy sweet that smells,
If not from my love's breath? The purple pride
4 Which on thy soft cheek for complexion dwells
In **my** love's **veins** thou hast too grossly dyed.'
The lily I condemnèd for thy hand,
And buds of marjoram had stol'n thy hair:
8 The roses fearfully on thorns did stand,
One blushing shame, another white despair;
A third, nor red nor white, had stol'n of both
And to his robb'ry had annex'd thy **breath**,
12 But, for his theft, in pride **of all** his **growth**
A vengeful canker eat him up to death.
　　More flowers I noted, yet I none could see
　　But sweet or colour it had stol'n from thee.

Let me not to the marriage of true minds
Admit impediments; love is not love
Which alters when it alteration finds,
Or bends with the remover to remove.
O no, it is an ever-fixèd mark
That looks on tempests and is never **shaken**;
It is the star to every **wand'ring** bark,
Whose **worth unknown**, although his height be taken.
Love's not Time's fool, though rosy lips and cheeks
Within his bending sickle's **compass** come:
Love alters not with his brief hours and weeks,
But bears it out **even** to **the edge of** doom.
    If this be **error** and upon me proved,
    I never writ, nor no man ever loved.

Accuse me thus: that I have scanted all
Wherein I should your great deserts repay,
Forgot upon your dearest love to call,
Whereto all bonds do tie me day by day;
That I have frequent been with unknown minds,
And given to time your own dear-purchased right
That I have **hoisted sail** to all the winds
Which should **transport me** farthest from your sight.
Book both my wilfulness and errors down,
And on just proof surmise accumulate;
Bring me within the level of your frown,
But shoot not at me in **your wake**nd hate;
　　Since my appeal says I did strive to prove
　　The constancy and virtue of your love.

Thy gift, thy tables, are within my brain
Full charactered with lasting memory,
Which shall above that idle rank remain
4   **Beyond all date**, even to eternity—
Or at the least, so long as brain and heart
Have faculty by nature to subsist;
Till each to razed oblivion yield his part
8   Of thee, thy record never can be missed.
That poor retention could not so much hold,
Nor need I tallies thy dear love to score;
Therefore to give them from me was I **bold**
12 To trust those tables that receive thee more.
    To keep an adjunct to remember thee
    Were to import forgetfulness in me.

O thou, my lovely boy, who in thy power
Dost hold Time's fickle glass, his sickle hour,
Who hast by waning grown, and therein show'st
Thy lovers withering as thy sweet self grow'st;
If Nature, **sovereign mistress over** **rack**,
As thou goest onwards, still will pluck thee back,
She keeps thee to this purpose, that her skill
May time disgrace and wretched minutes kill.
Yet fear her, O thou minion of her **pleasure**;
She may detain, but not still keep, her treasure.
  Her audit, though delayed, answered must be,
  And **her quietus** is **to render** thee.

In the old age black was not counted fair,
Or if it were, it bore not beauty's name;
But now is black beauty's successive heir,
And **beauty** slander'd with a bastard shame:
For since each hand hath put on nature's power,
Fairing the foul with art's false **borrowed** face,
Sweet beauty hath **no name, no** holy **bower,**
But is profaned, if not lives in disgrace.
Therefore my mistress' brows are raven black,
Her eyes so suited, and they mourners seem
At such who, not born fair, no beauty lack,
Sland'ring creation with a false esteem:
    Yet **so** they mourn, **our** **becoming** of their woe,
    That every tongue **says** beauty should look so.

How oft, when thou, my music, music play'st,
Upon that blessèd wood whose **motion sounds**
With thy sweet fingers, when thou gently sway'st
4   The wiry concord that mine ear confounds,
Do I envy those jacks that nimble leap
To kiss **the tender inward of** thy **hand,**
Whilst my poor **lips,** which should that harvest reap,
8   At the wood's **boldness** by thee blushing stand.
To be so tickled, they would change their state
And situation with those dancing chips
O'er whom thy fingers walk with gentle gait,
12   Making dead wood more blest than living lips.
    Since saucy jacks so happy are in this,
    Give them thy fingers, me thy lips to kiss.

The expense of spirit in a waste of shame
Is lust in action, and till action, lust
Is perjured, murderous, bloody, full of blame,
4   Savage, **extreme**, rude, cruel, not to **trust**,
Enjoy'd no sooner but despisèd straight,
Past reason hunted, and no sooner had,
Past reason hated as a swallow'd bait
8   On purpose laid **to make the** taker mad;
Mad in pursuit and in possession so,
Had, **having**, and in quest to have, **extreme**,
A bliss in proof, and proved, a very woe,
12   Before, a joy proposed, behind, a dream.
  All this the world well knows; yet none knows well
  To shun the heaven that leads men to this hell.

My mistress' eyes are nothing like the sun;
Coral is far more red than her lips' red;
If snow be white, why then her breasts are dun;
If hairs be wires, black wires grow on her head.
I have seen roses damasked, red and white,
But **no such roses** see I in her cheeks,
And in some perfumes is there more delight
Than in the breath that from my mistress reeks.
I love to hear her speak, yet well I know
That music hath a far more pleasing sound.
I grant I never saw a goddess go;
My mistress when she walks treads on the ground:
And yet, by heaven, I think my love as rare
As any she belied with false compare.

So, now I have confessed that he is thine,
And I myself am mortgaged to thy will,
Myself I'll forfeit, so that other mine
4   Thou wilt restore to be my comfort still.
But thou wilt not, nor he will nor be free,
For thou art covetous, and he is kind;
He learned but surety-like to write for me
8   Under that bond that him as fast doth bind.
The statute of thy beauty thou wilt take,
Thou usurer that put'st forth all to use,
And sue a friend came debtor for my sake;
12 So him I lose through my unkind abuse.
    Him have I lost; thou hast both him and me;
    He pays the whole, and yet am I not free.

Whoever hath her wish, thou hast thy 'Will,'
And 'Will' to boot, and 'Will' in overplus;
More than enough am I that vex thee still,
To thy sweet will making addition thus.
Wilt thou, whose will is large and spacious,
Not once vouchsafe to hide my will in thine?
Shall will in others seem right gracious,
And in my will no fair acceptance shine?
The sea all water, yet receives rain still
And in abundance addeth to his store;
So thou, being rich in 'Will,' add to thy 'Will'
One will of mine, to make thy large 'Will' more.
    Let 'no' unkind, no fair beseechers kill;
    Think all but one, and me in that one 'Will.'

If thy soul check thee that I come so near,
Swear to thy blind soul that I was thy 'Will,'
And will, thy soul knows, is admitted there;
Thus far for love my love-suit, sweet, fulfil.
'Will' will fulfil the treasure of thy love,
Ay, fill it full with wills, and my will one.
In things of great receipt with ease we prove
Among a number one is reckoned none.
Then in the number let me pass untold,
Though in thy store's account I one must be;
For nothing **hold me**, so it please thee hold
That nothing me, a something, sweet, **to** thee.
    Make but my name thy love, and love that still,
    And then thou lov'st me, for **my name** is 'Will.'

Thou blind fool, Love, what dost thou to mine eyes
That they behold and see not what they see?
They know what beauty is, see where it lies,
4   Yet what the best is take the worst to be.
If eyes corrupt by over-partial looks
Be **anchored** in the bay where all men ride,
Why of eyes' falsehood hast thou forgèd hooks,
8   Whereto the judgment of my heart is tied?
Why should my heart think that a several plot,
Which my heart knows the wide world's common place?
Or mine eyes seeing this, say this is not,
12   To put fair truth upon so foul a face?
         In things right true my heart and eyes have erred,
         And to this false plague are they now transferred.

When my love swears that she is made of truth
I do believe **her**, though I know she lies,
That she might think me some untutored youth,
Unlearnèd in the world's false **subtilties**.
Thus vainly thinking that she thinks me young,
Although she knows my days are past the best,
Simply I credit her false-speaking tongue:
On both sides thus is simple truth suppressed.
But wherefore says she not she is unjust?
And wherefore say not I that I am **old**?
O, love's best habit is in seeming trust,
And age in love **loves** not to have years told.
  Therefore I lie with her and she **with me**,
  And in our faults by lies we flattered be.

O, call not me to justify the wrong
That thy unkindness lays upon my heart;
Wound me not with thine eye but with thy **tongue**.
4　Use power with power **and** slay me not by art.
Tell me thou lov'st **elsewhere**, but in my sight,
Dear heart, forbear to glance thine eye aside:
What need'st thou wound with cunning when thy might
8　Is more than my o'erpress'd defence can bide?
Let me excuse thee: 'Ah, my love well knows
Her pretty looks have been mine enemies,
And therefore from my face she **turn**s my foes,
12　That they elsewhere might dart their injuries.'
　　　Yet do not so; but since I am near slain,
　　　Kill me outright with looks and rid my pain.

In faith, I do not love thee with mine eyes,
For they in thee **a thousand** errors note;
But 'tis my heart that loves what they despise,
4   Who in despite of view is pleased to dote.
Nor are mine ears with thy tongue's tune delighted,
Nor **tender** feeling to base touches prone,
Nor taste, nor smell, desire to be invited
8   To any sensual feast with thee alone.
But my five wits nor my five senses can
Dissuade one foolish heart from serving thee,
Who **leaves unsway**ed **the likeness** of a man,
12   Thy proud heart's slave and vassal wretch to be.
    Only my plague thus far I count my gain,
    That she that makes me sin awards me pain.

Love is my sin and thy dear virtue hate,
Hate of my sin, grounded on sinful loving.
O, but with mine compare thou thine own state,
4   And thou shalt find it merits not reproving;
Or if it do, not **from those lips** of thine,
That have profaned **the**ir **scarlet** ornaments
And sealed false bonds of love as oft as mine,
8   Robbed others' **beds**' revenues of their rents.
Be it lawful I love thee, as thou lov'st those
Whom thine eyes woo as mine importune thee.
Root pity in thy heart, that, when it **grow**,
12 Thy pity may deserve to pitied be.
    If thou dost seek to have what thou dost hide,
    By self-example mayst thou be denied.

Those lips that Love's own hand did make
Breathed **forth the sound** that said 'I hate'
To me that languished for her sake.
4   But when she saw my woeful state,
Straight in her heart did mercy come,
Chiding that tongue that ever sweet
Was used in giving gentle doom,
8   And taught it thus **anew** to greet:
'I hate' she **alter'd** with an end
That followed it **as gentle day**
Doth follow night, who, like a fiend
12 From heaven to hell is flown away.
    'I hate' from hate away she threw,
    And saved my life, saying 'not you.'

O, from what power hast thou this powerful might
With insufficiency my heart to sway?
To make me give the lie to my true sight
4   And swear **that bright**ness doth not grace the day?
Whence hast thou this **becoming of things** ill
That **in the very refuse** of thy deeds
There is **such strength** and warrantise of skill
8   That in my mind thy worst all best exceeds?
Who taught thee how to make me love thee more,
The more I hear and see just cause of hate?
O, though I love what others do abhor,
12 With others thou shouldst not abhor my state.
    If thy unworthiness raised love in me,
    More worthy I to be beloved of thee.

Working Note

I stripped Shakespeare's sonnets bare to the "nets" to make the space of the poems open, porous, possible—a divergent elsewhere. When we write poems, the history of poetry is with us, pre-inscribed in the white of the page; when we read or write poems, we do it with or against this palimpsest.

—Jen Bervin

NETS was designed and typeset by Anna Moschovakis and Jen Bervin using Caslon for the text and Hoefler Text for the numbers. Fifteen years after its 2004 publication, the 11th printing, consisting of 1500 copies, was printed offset and bound at McNaughton & Gunn, with covers printed letterpress at the UDP studio.

Ugly Duckling Presse
The Old American Can Factory
232 Third Street #E-303
Brooklyn, NY 11215

Please see our full catalog at
uglyducklingpresse.org